LIVING IN AMAZING GRACE—
The Nature of God

Retreat/Group Companion
WORKBOOK

RICHARD T. CASE

Dedication/Acknowledgements

We often sing at church, the beautiful Hymn—*Amazing Grace*, penned by John Newton. He is said to have written it as a heartfelt expression to God in 1772. It was inspired by a pivotal time in his life after surviving a shipwreck. Newton was involved in the slave trade but would go on to regret his actions and became a priest who advocated for the abolishment of slavery.

We tend to associate this term—amazing grace—with our salvation experience in being born again, due to God's grace toward us who do not deserve based upon being perfect or cannot attain a relationship with God by ourselves. As we have explored further in the Word about the truth, the breadth and fullness of Grace, we have learned of the deeper profound truths of living in Grace. We wish to dedicate this course to and thank my wife, Linda, who has learned these deeper truths and lived them out in our marriage and family. Further, we dedicate this to our ministry leaders who have personally demonstrated this life.

We experience this fullness of Grace because God's nature is Grace—all His nature is Grace. This includes redemption, favor, freedom, goodness, pleasantness, overcoming, miraculous, and leading us into the experience of this fullness. We learned that our experience of Grace is not automatic, but there are conditions to our receiving and experiencing the Grace of God in our everyday lives. And, as we experience this, we are to give it away—be conduits to others of this amazing grace available to all. Linda and the leaders understand this Grace, are living it out and giving it away. It is a joy for all of us. Thank you, Linda and team. An honor.

These leaders are:

Jake & Mary Beckel
Joe & Leigh Bogar
Heath & Rebecca Cardie
Rich & Janet Cocchiaro
Larry & Sherry Collett
Scott & Kristen Cornell
David & Melissa Dunkel
Tom & Susanne Ewing
Rick & Kelly Ferris
Joel & Christina Gunn
Scott & Terry Hitchcock
Rick & Nancy Hoover
Tad & Monica Jones
Ed & Becky Kobel
Don & Rachelle Light
Chris & Heidi May
Terry & Josephine Noetzel
Towanda Norton
Steve & Carolyn Van Ooteghem
Preston & Lynda Pitts
Dan & Kathy Rocconi
Bob & Keri Rockwell
John & Michelle Santaferraro
Allyson & Denny Weinberg
Neal & Kathy Weisenburger

LIVING IN AMAZING GRACE—THE NATURE OF GOD COMPANION WORKBOOK
PUBLISHED BY LIVING WATERS—ABIDE MINISTRIES
7615 Lemon Gulch Way
Castle Rock, CO 80108

ISBN: 979-8-218-24470-5

Publisher's Cataloging-in-Publication data

Names:
Title:
Description: .
Identifiers: ISBN | LCCN
Subjects:

Printed in the United States of America 2024 — 2nd ed

TABLE OF CONTENTS

What is grace? Who is grace? What does this mean regarding why it is so important to understand the fullness of grace versus grace just being a ticket to heaven?

Read Revelation 1:3–6:

3 Blessed is the one who reads aloud the words of this prophecy, and blessed are those who hear, and who keep what is written in it, for the time is near.

Greeting to the Seven Churches
4 John to the seven churches that are in Asia:
Grace to you and peace from him who is and who was and who is to come, and from the seven spirits who are before his throne, 5 and from Jesus Christ the faithful witness, the firstborn of the dead, and the ruler of kings on earth.

To him who loves us and has freed us from our sins by his blood 6 and made us a kingdom, priests to his God and Father, to him be glory and dominion forever and ever. Amen.

What are situations, relationship issues, personal issues for which you are needing to understand, receive, and then extend grace?

"Grace is majesty, magnificence, splendor, truth—it is the way to live with Him."

From the following two verses, what are the biblical definitions of grace? What do these mean for us? Why is this important to understand as we learn of grace?

Read Psalm 45:1–8:

Your Throne, O God, Is Forever
To the choirmaster: according to Lilies. A Maskil[a] of the Sons of Korah; a love song.
45 My heart overflows with a pleasing theme;
   I address my verses to the king;
   my tongue is like the pen of a ready scribe.
² You are the most handsome of the sons of men;
   grace is poured upon your lips;
   therefore God has blessed you forever.
³ Gird your sword on your thigh, O mighty one,
   in your splendor and majesty!
⁴ In your majesty ride out victoriously
   for the cause of truth and meekness and righteousness;
   let your right hand teach you awesome deeds!
⁵ Your arrows are sharp
   in the heart of the king's enemies;
   the peoples fall under you.
⁶ Your throne, O God, is forever and ever.
   The scepter of your kingdom is a scepter of uprightness;
⁷   you have loved righteousness and hated wickedness.
Therefore God, your God, has anointed you
   with the oil of gladness beyond your companions;
⁸   your robes are all fragrant with myrrh and aloes and cassia.
From ivory palaces stringed instruments make you glad;

> **Read John 1:14–18:**
>
> 14 And the Word became flesh and dwelt among us, and we have seen his glory, glory as of the only Son[a] from the Father, full of grace and truth. 15 (John bore witness about him, and cried out, "This was he of whom I said, 'He who comes after me ranks before me, because he was before me.'") 16 For from his fullness we have all received, grace upon grace.[b] 17 For the law was given through Moses; grace and truth came through Jesus Christ. 18 No one has ever seen God; the only God,[c] who is at the Father's side,[d] he has made him known.

LESSON 1:
WHAT IS GRACE? DESCRIPTION OF THE NATURE OF GOD.

Why does all of mankind need grace? What is the problem for us all? How then did Christ resolve this problem? On what basis does this define grace?

Read Romans 3:21–26:

The Righteousness of God Through Faith

21 But now the righteousness of God has been manifested apart from the law, although the Law and the Prophets bear witness to it— 22 the righteousness of God through faith in Jesus Christ for all who believe. For there is no distinction: 23 for all have sinned and fall short of the glory of God, 24 and are justified by his grace as a gift, through the redemption that is in Christ Jesus, 25 whom God put forward as a propitiation by his blood, to be received by faith. This was to show God's righteousness, because in his divine forbearance he had passed over former sins. 26 It was to show his righteousness at the present time, so that he might be just and the justifier of the one who has faith in Jesus.

What is God's purpose for extending us grace? What does that mean for our lives? What then are we to experience? How can we experience this?

> **Read 2 Timothy 1:8–12:**
>
> [8] Therefore do not be ashamed of the testimony about our Lord, nor of me his prisoner, but share in suffering for the gospel by the power of God, [9] who saved us and called us to[a] a holy calling, not because of our works but because of his own purpose and grace, which he gave us in Christ Jesus before the ages began,[b] [10] and which now has been manifested through the appearing of our Savior Christ Jesus, who abolished death and brought life and immortality to light through the gospel, [11] for which I was appointed a preacher and apostle and teacher, [12] which is why I suffer as I do. But I am not ashamed, for I know whom I have believed, and I am convinced that he is able to guard until that day what has been entrusted to me.[c]

____

____

____

____

____

With Christ's nature of grace when He raised us up with Him, what are the four benefits to us that He fulfilled at the cross? What do these practically mean to us, and why is this so important?

Read Colossians 2:11–15:

[11] In him also you were circumcised with a circumcision made without hands, by putting off the body of the flesh, by the circumcision of Christ, [12] having been buried with him in baptism, in which you were also raised with him through faith in the powerful working of God, who raised him from the dead. [13] And you, who were dead in your trespasses and the uncircumcision of your flesh, God made alive together with him, having forgiven us all our trespasses, [14] by canceling the record of debt that stood against us with its legal demands. This he set aside, nailing it to the cross. [15] He disarmed the rulers and authorities[a] and put them to open shame, by triumphing over them in him.[b]

____

____

____

____

____

From the following two sets of verses, what are other wonderful benefits of living in God's grace? What does this practically mean regarding how we live our life—including relationships toward others?

Read Romans 8:1–2:

Life in the Spirit

8 There is therefore now no condemnation for those who are in Christ Jesus. [a] 2 For the law of the Spirit of life has set you[b] free in Christ Jesus from the law of sin and death.

____

____

____

____

____

Read John 5:24:

24 Truly, truly, I say to you, whoever hears my word and believes him who sent me has eternal life. He does not come into judgment, but has passed from death to life.

____

____

____

____

____

From the following two sets of verses: As we experience grace, what is to characterize our life? What does this mean, and how then shall we expect to live all the time? What is the condition to living this way? Why?

Read Galatians 4:21–5:1:

Example of Hagar and Sarah

21 Tell me, you who desire to be under the law, do you not listen to the law? 22 For it is written that Abraham had two sons, one by a slave woman and one by a free woman. 23 But the son of the slave was born according to the flesh, while the son of the free woman was born through promise. 24 Now this may be interpreted allegorically: these women are two covenants. One is from Mount Sinai, bearing children for slavery; she is Hagar. 25 Now Hagar is Mount Sinai in Arabia;[a] she corresponds to the present Jerusalem, for she is in slavery with her children. 26 But the Jerusalem above is free, and she is our mother. 27 For it is written,

"Rejoice, O barren one who does not bear;
    break forth and cry aloud, you who are not in labor!
For the children of the desolate one will be more
    than those of the one who has a husband."

28 Now you,[b] brothers, like Isaac, are children of promise. 29 But just as at that time he who was born according to the flesh persecuted him who was born according to the Spirit, so also it is now. 30 But what does the Scripture say? "Cast out the slave woman and her son, for the son of the slave woman shall not inherit with the son of the free woman." 31 So, brothers, we are not children of the slave but of the free woman.

Christ Has Set Us Free

5 For freedom Christ has set us free; stand firm therefore, and do not submit again to a yoke of slavery.

Read John 8:28–32; 36:

28 So Jesus said to them, "When you have lifted up the Son of Man, then you will know that I am he, and that I do nothing on my own authority, but speak just as the Father taught me. 29 And he who sent me is with me. He has not left me alone, for I always do the things that are pleasing to him." 30 As he was saying these things, many believed in him.

The Truth Will Set You Free
31 So Jesus said to the Jews who had believed him, "If you abide in my word, you are truly my disciples, 32 and you will know the truth, and the truth will set you free."

36 So if the Son sets you free, you will be free indeed.

____

____

____

____

____

To understand grace, we again need to understand the question: Who is grace and peace? Why is this fundamental understanding so critical to us receiving and living in grace?

Read Galatians 1:3–5:

3 Grace to you and peace from God our Father and the Lord Jesus Christ, 4 who gave himself for our sins to deliver us from the present evil age, according to the will of our God and Father, 5 to whom be the glory forever and ever. Amen.

____

____

____

____

Is it possible that though Christ is grace and has extended us grace, we might not experience it as a believer? Why does this happen, and what then is the consequence? Why is this so important for us to learn?

Read Galatians 2:17–21:

[17] But if, in our endeavor to be justified in Christ, we too were found to be sinners, is Christ then a servant of sin? Certainly not! [18] For if I rebuild what I tore down, I prove myself to be a transgressor. [19] For through the law I died to the law, so that I might live to God. [20] I have been crucified with Christ. It is no longer I who live, but Christ who lives in me. And the life I now live in the flesh I live by faith in the Son of God, who loved me and gave himself for me. [21] I do not nullify the grace of God, for if righteousness[a] were through the law, then Christ died for no purpose.

LESSON 1:
WHAT IS GRACE? DESCRIPTION OF THE NATURE OF GOD.

What happened that all mankind requires grace? What did Christ do to resolve this and bring about His grace? Thus, what is the central truth about what is necessary to receive His grace? Why then is this so critical to how we live?

Read Romans 5:12–21:

Death in Adam, Life in Christ

12 Therefore, just as sin came into the world through one man, and death through sin, and so death spread to all men[a] because all sinned— 13 for sin indeed was in the world before the law was given, but sin is not counted where there is no law. 14 Yet death reigned from Adam to Moses, even over those whose sinning was not like the transgression of Adam, who was a type of the one who was to come.

15 But the free gift is not like the trespass. For if many died through one man's trespass, much more have the grace of God and the free gift by the grace of that one man Jesus Christ abounded for many. 16 And the free gift is not like the result of that one man's sin. For the judgment following one trespass brought condemnation, but the free gift following many trespasses brought justification. 17 For if, because of one man's trespass, death reigned through that one man, much more will those who receive the abundance of grace and the free gift of righteousness reign in life through the one man Jesus Christ.

18 Therefore, as one trespass[b] led to condemnation for all men, so one act of righteousness[c] leads to justification and life for all men. 19 For as by the one man's disobedience the many were made sinners, so by the one man's obedience the many will be made righteous. 20 Now the law came in to increase the trespass, but where sin increased, grace abounded all the more, 21 so that, as sin reigned in death, grace also might reign through righteousness leading to eternal life through Jesus Christ our Lord.

Since Christ is grace, what is necessary for us to receive it and live it out? How much of grace can we expect, and why then is this so important?

> **Read 1 Corinthians 14:29:**
>
> [29] Let two or three prophets speak, and let the others weigh what is said.

____

____

____

____

____

From the following two sets of verses, if you attempt to live the life of grace on your own, what happens? Then, what is necessary for us to live the life of grace? How do we live that way practically?

> **Read Romans 8:3–5:**
>
> [3] For God has done what the law, weakened by the flesh, could not do. By sending his own Son in the likeness of sinful flesh and for sin,[a] he condemned sin in the flesh, [4] in order that the righteous requirement of the law might be fulfilled in us, who walk not according to the flesh but according to the Spirit. [5] For those who live according to the flesh set their minds on the things of the flesh, but those who live according to the Spirit set their minds on the things of the Spirit.

____

____

____

____

____

Read John 14:25–31:

[25] "These things I have spoken to you while I am still with you. [26] But the Helper, the Holy Spirit, whom the Father will send in my name, he will teach you all things and bring to your remembrance all that I have said to you. [27] Peace I leave with you; my peace I give to you. Not as the world gives do I give to you. Let not your hearts be troubled, neither let them be afraid. [28] You heard me say to you, 'I am going away, and I will come to you.' If you loved me, you would have rejoiced, because I am going to the Father, for the Father is greater than I. [29] And now I have told you before it takes place, so that when it does take place you may believe. [30] I will no longer talk much with you, for the ruler of this world is coming. He has no claim on me, [31] but I do as the Father has commanded me, so that the world may know that I love the Father. Rise, let us go from here.

What is the basis of grace? What is the heart of God toward all who are His children? What does that mean then for what we can expect? Why is that?

Read Genesis 12:1–3:

The Call of Abram
12 Now the LORD said[a] to Abram, "Go from your country[b] and your kindred and your father's house to the land that I will show you. [2] And I will make of you a great nation, and I will bless you and make your name great, so that you will be a blessing. [3] I will bless those who bless you, and him who dishonors you I will curse, and in you all the families of the earth shall be blessed."[c]

____

____

____

____

____

What is necessary for us to receive God's Covenant blessings? What does that look like practically for how we follow God?

Read Deuteronomy 28:1–14:

Blessings for Obedience
28 "And if you faithfully obey the voice of the LORD your God, being careful to do all his commandments that I command you today, the LORD your God will set you high above all the nations of the earth. [2] And all these blessings shall come upon you and overtake you, if you obey the voice of the LORD your God.

[3] Blessed shall you be in the city, and blessed shall you be in the field. [4] Blessed shall be the fruit of your womb and the fruit of your ground and the fruit of your cattle, the increase of your herds and the young of your flock. [5] Blessed shall be your basket and your kneading bowl. [6] Blessed shall you be when you come in, and blessed shall you be when you go out.

> [7] "The LORD will cause your enemies who rise against you to be defeated before you. They shall come out against you one way and flee before you seven ways. [8] The LORD will command the blessing on you in your barns and in all that you undertake. And he will bless you in the land that the LORD your God is giving you. [9] The LORD will establish you as a people holy to himself, as he has sworn to you, if you keep the commandments of the LORD your God and walk in his ways. [10] And all the peoples of the earth shall see that you are called by the name of the LORD, and they shall be afraid of you. [11] And the LORD will make you abound in prosperity, in the fruit of your womb and in the fruit of your livestock and in the fruit of your ground, within the land that the LORD swore to your fathers to give you. [12] The LORD will open to you his good treasury, the heavens, to give the rain to your land in its season and to bless all the work of your hands. And you shall lend to many nations, but you shall not borrow. [13] And the LORD will make you the head and not the tail, and you shall only go up and not down, if you obey the commandments of the LORD your God, which I command you today, being careful to do them, [14] and if you do not turn aside from any of the words that I command you today, to the right hand or to the left, to go after other gods to serve them.

From the following two sets of verses, since God promised us Covenant life, what promises did Christ specifically give us so that we experience the life of grace? What can we then expect and why?

Read John 10:10:

[10] The thief comes only to steal and kill and destroy. I came that they may have life and have it abundantly.

____

____

____

____

____

Read Isaiah 61:1–4:

The Year of the LORD'S Favor
61 The Spirit of the Lord God is upon me,
   because the LORD has anointed me
to bring good news to the poor;[a]
   he has sent me to bind up the brokenhearted,
to proclaim liberty to the captives,
   and the opening of the prison to those who are bound;[b]
[2] to proclaim the year of the LORD'S favor,
   and the day of vengeance of our God;
   to comfort all who mourn;
[3] to grant to those who mourn in Zion—
   to give them a beautiful headdress instead of ashes,
the oil of gladness instead of mourning,
   the garment of praise instead of a faint spirit;
that they may be called oaks of righteousness,

> the planting of the LORD, that he may be glorified.[c]
>
> [4] They shall build up the ancient ruins;
>   they shall raise up the former devastations;
> they shall repair the ruined cities,
>   the devastations of many generations.

____

____

____

____

____

A significant part of our life is spent experiencing difficulty, hard circumstances, and negative consequences—including loss. As part of God's grace, what does He promise even in these conditions? What does that mean for our life of grace? Why is this so important to understand?

Read Deuteronomy 30:1–10:

Repentance and Forgiveness

30 "And when all these things come upon you, the blessing and the curse, which I have set before you, and you call them to mind among all the nations where the LORD your God has driven you, [2] and return to the LORD your God, you and your children, and obey his voice in all that I command you today, with all your heart and with all your soul, [3] then the LORD your God will restore your fortunes and have mercy on you, and he will gather you again from all the peoples where the LORD your God has scattered you. [4] If your outcasts are in the uttermost parts of heaven, from there the LORD your God will gather you, and from there he will take you. [5] And the LORD your God will bring you into the land that your fathers possessed, that you may possess it. And he will make you more prosperous and numerous than your fathers. [6] And the LORD your God will circumcise your heart and the heart of your offspring, so that you will love the LORD your God with all your heart and with all your soul, that you may live. [7] And the LORD your God will put all these curses on your foes and enemies

> who persecuted you. [8] And you shall again obey the voice of the LORD and keep all his commandments that I command you today. [9] The LORD your God will make you abundantly prosperous in all the work of your hand, in the fruit of your womb and in the fruit of your cattle and in the fruit of your ground. For the LORD will again take delight in prospering you, as he took delight in your fathers, [10] when you obey the voice of the LORD your God, to keep his commandments and his statutes that are written in this Book of the Law, when you turn to the LORD your God with all your heart and with all your soul.

____

____

____

____

God further says that if you have a heart to go, He can prevent you from experiencing some trouble. The life of grace includes protection. From the following two sets of verses: What protection is promised? What does this mean to our life, and what is the benefit to us living under this protection?

> **Read Psalm 5:11–12:**
>
> [11] But let all who take refuge in you rejoice;
>   let them ever sing for joy,
> and spread your protection over them,
>   that those who love your name may exult in you.
> [12] For you bless the righteous, O LORD;
>   you cover him with favor as with a shield.

____

____

____

____

Read Psalm 84:11–12:

[11] For the LORD God is a sun and shield;
　　the LORD bestows favor and honor.
No good thing does he withhold
　　from those who walk uprightly.
[12] O LORD of hosts,
　　blessed is the one who trusts in you!

____

____

____

____

____

Christ reminds us that He is grace, and He desires to have us live with Him—living the life of grace and experiencing all its benefits. What is His promise for us to experience this?

Read 2 Thessalonians 1:11–12:

[11] To this end we always pray for you, that our God may make you worthy of his calling and may fulfill every resolve for good and every work of faith by his power, [12] so that the name of our Lord Jesus may be glorified in you, and you in him, according to the grace of our God and the Lord Jesus Christ.

____

____

____

____

____

LESSON 2:
WHAT ARE THE CHARACTERISTICS OF GRACE?

When God lifts up veils—opens up new understanding—what does He do for us (vs. 18) that changes us? In what way does God fulfill this change? Why is this necessary? What is the outcome? What is true where the Spirit of the Lord is? Why is this important?

Read 2 Corinthians 3:16–18:

[16] But when one[a] turns to the Lord, the veil is removed. [17] Now the Lord[b] is the Spirit, and where the Spirit of the Lord is, there is freedom. [18] And we all, with unveiled face, beholding the glory of the Lord,[c] are being transformed into the same image from one degree of glory to another.[d] For this comes from the Lord who is the Spirit.

> "He says that His nature of grace will transform your experience of life step by step by step."

Why are we called to freedom? On what basis can we live in freedom? Thus, when is freedom available to us? Why is this important?

Read Galatians 5:1; 13:

Christ Has Set Us Free

5 For freedom Christ has set us free; stand firm therefore, and do not submit again to a yoke of slavery.

[13] For you were called to freedom, brothers. Only do not use your freedom as an opportunity for the flesh, but through love serve one another.

LESSON 2:
WHAT ARE THE CHARACTERISTICS OF GRACE?

____

____

____

____

____

From the following two sets of verses, from Jesus' instruction on prayer and the truths of Ephesians, as we live in freedom, in His Kingdom, in His will, what is important for us to continue to live in freedom? What does that mean for how we live?

Read Luke 11:1–4:

The Lord's Prayer

11 Now Jesus[a] was praying in a certain place, and when he finished, one of his disciples said to him, "Lord, teach us to pray, as John taught his disciples." [2] And he said to them, "When you pray, say:

"Father, hallowed be your name.
Your kingdom come.
[3] Give us each day our daily bread,[b]
[4] and forgive us our sins,
    for we ourselves forgive everyone who is indebted to us.
And lead us not into temptation."

____

____

____

____

LESSON 2:
WHAT ARE THE CHARACTERISTICS OF GRACE?

Read Ephesians 4:29–32:

29 Let no corrupting talk come out of your mouths, but only such as is good for building up, as fits the occasion, that it may give grace to those who hear. 30 And do not grieve the Holy Spirit of God, by whom you were sealed for the day of redemption. 31 Let all bitterness and wrath and anger and clamor and slander be put away from you, along with all malice. 32 Be kind to one another, tenderhearted, forgiving one another, as God in Christ forgave you.

____

____

____

____

____

Why are we called not to judge others? How do we practically experience this when others are difficult or in conflict with us?

Read James 4:11–12:

11 Do not speak evil against one another, brothers.[a] The one who speaks against a brother or judges his brother, speaks evil against the law and judges the law. But if you judge the law, you are not a doer of the law but a judge. 12 There is only one lawgiver and judge, he who is able to save and to destroy. But who are you to judge your neighbor?

____

____

____

____

____

Why are we to avoid going to law? What does that mean that we go to "I should," or "You should"? Why is this so important for living in freedom?

Read Galatians 5:13–15:

13 For you were called to freedom, brothers. Only do not use your freedom as an opportunity for the flesh, but through love serve one another. 14 For the whole law is fulfilled in one word: "You shall love your neighbor as yourself." 15 But if you bite and devour one another, watch out that you are not consumed by one another.

When others are coming against you, what are you called to do? Why? How do you do this when it is so difficult not to engage in the battle or conflict?

Read 2 Corinthians 12:19–21:

19 Have you been thinking all along that we have been defending ourselves to you? It is in the sight of God that we have been speaking in Christ, and all for your upbuilding, beloved. 20 For I fear that perhaps when I come I may find you not as I wish, and that you may find me not as you wish—that perhaps there may be quarreling, jealousy, anger, hostility, slander, gossip, conceit, and disorder. 21 I fear that when I come again my God may humble me before you, and I may have to mourn over many of those who sinned earlier and have not repented of the impurity, sexual immorality, and sensuality that they have practiced.

In what way can we make the life of freedom given to us by God become vain (of no value)? Why is it so important for us to realize this?

Read 2 Corinthians 6:1–3:

6 Working together with him, then, we appeal to you not to receive the grace of God in vain. [2] For he says,

"In a favorable time I listened to you,
    and in a day of salvation I have helped you."

Behold, now is the favorable time; behold, now is the day of salvation. [3] We put no obstacle in anyone's way, so that no fault may be found with our ministry,

---

____

____

____

____

____

As we walk with God, what is His purpose for us? How can we stay in freedom while He is transforming us?

Read Hebrews 13:7–16:

[7] Remember your leaders, those who spoke to you the word of God. Consider the outcome of their way of life, and imitate their faith. [8] Jesus Christ is the same yesterday and today and forever. [9] Do not be led away by diverse and strange teachings, for it is good for the heart to be strengthened by grace, not by foods, which have not benefited those devoted to them. [10] We have an altar from which those who serve the tent[a] have no right to eat. [11] For the bodies of those animals whose blood is brought into the holy places by the high priest as a sacrifice for sin are burned outside the camp. [12] So Jesus also suffered outside the gate in order to sanctify the people through his own blood. [13] Therefore let us go to him outside the camp and bear the reproach he endured. [14] For here we have no lasting city, but we seek the city that is to come. [15] Through him then let

---

> us continually offer up a sacrifice of praise to God, that is, the fruit of lips that acknowledge his name. [16] Do not neglect to do good and to share what you have, for such sacrifices are pleasing to God.

____

____

____

____

____

Since grace is Christ and Christ is living in us, what does He promise when we experience trouble and difficult circumstances? What does that mean in relation to how we follow and live in Christ? Why?

> **Read 2 Corinthians 4:7–15:**
>
> Treasure in Jars of Clay
>
> [7] But we have this treasure in jars of clay, to show that the surpassing power belongs to God and not to us. [8] We are afflicted in every way, but not crushed; perplexed, but not driven to despair; [9] persecuted, but not forsaken; struck down, but not destroyed; [10] always carrying in the body the death of Jesus, so that the life of Jesus may also be manifested in our bodies. [11] For we who live are always being given over to death for Jesus' sake, so that the life of Jesus also may be manifested in our mortal flesh. [12] So death is at work in us, but life in you.
>
> [13] Since we have the same spirit of faith according to what has been written, "I believed, and so I spoke," we also believe, and so we also speak, [14] knowing that he who raised the Lord Jesus will raise us also with Jesus and bring us with you into his presence. [15] For it is all for your sake, so that as grace extends to more and more people it may increase thanksgiving, to the glory of God.

____

____

____

____

LESSON 2:
WHAT ARE THE CHARACTERISTICS OF GRACE?

From the following two sets of verses, since we live in the world, what are we going to experience? Why does grace not exempt us from this? What is the good news about grace that we are going to experience? Why is this so important for us?

> **Read John 16:33:**
>
> 33 I have said these things to you, that in me you may have peace. In the world you will have tribulation. But take heart; I have overcome the world."

____

____

____

____

____

When you have trouble, go to God and ask: What do You have to say about this? Grace confirms that He has the answer because He has overcome the world of trouble. He's got this. It's His nature. He has already overcome it and will get you the answer if you have a heart to go with Him. Trust and enjoy His resolution and overcoming.

> **Read Revelation 3:20–21:**
>
> 20 Behold, I stand at the door and knock. If anyone hears my voice and opens the door, I will come in to him and eat with him, and he with me. 21 The one who conquers, I will grant him to sit with me on my throne, as I also conquered and sat down with my Father on his throne.

____

____

____

____

From the following four sets of verses, we see that lovingkindness means God's loyalty to the Covenant. What is the Covenant? What are the benefits of living in Him and receiving His Covenant blessings? What does it mean that He is loyal to that for us? What then shall we expect?

Read Psalm 31:19–21:

19 Oh, how abundant is your goodness,
  which you have stored up for those who fear you
and worked for those who take refuge in you,
  in the sight of the children of mankind!
20 In the cover of your presence you hide them
  from the plots of men;
you store them in your shelter
  from the strife of tongues.
21 Blessed be the LORD,
  for he has wondrously shown his steadfast love to me
  when I was in a besieged city.

Read Psalm 65:4–8; 11–13:

4 Blessed is the one you choose and bring near,
  to dwell in your courts!
We shall be satisfied with the goodness of your house,
  the holiness of your temple!
5 By awesome deeds you answer us with righteousness,
  O God of our salvation,
the hope of all the ends of the earth
  and of the farthest seas;
6 the one who by his strength established the mountains,
  being girded with might;
7 who stills the roaring of the seas,
  the roaring of their waves,
  the tumult of the peoples,
8 so that those who dwell at the ends of the earth are in awe at your signs.
You make the going out of the morning and the evening to shout for joy.

Read Psalm 16:5–11:

[5] The LORD is my chosen portion and my cup;
  you hold my lot.
[6] The lines have fallen for me in pleasant places;
  indeed, I have a beautiful inheritance.
[7] I bless the LORD who gives me counsel;
  in the night also my heart instructs me.[a]
[8] I have set the LORD always before me;
  because he is at my right hand, I shall not be shaken.
[9] Therefore my heart is glad, and my whole being[b] rejoices;
  my flesh also dwells secure.
[10] For you will not abandon my soul to Sheol,
  or let your holy one see corruption.[c]
[11] You make known to me the path of life;
  in your presence there is fullness of joy;
  at your right hand are pleasures forevermore.

____

____

____

____

____

Read Proverbs 3:13–18:

Blessed Is the One Who Finds Wisdom

13 Blessed is the one who finds wisdom,
   and the one who gets understanding,
14 for the gain from her is better than gain from silver
   and her profit better than gold.
15 She is more precious than jewels,
   and nothing you desire can compare with her.
16 Long life is in her right hand;
   in her left hand are riches and honor.
17 Her ways are ways of pleasantness,
   and all her paths are peace.
18 She is a tree of life to those who lay hold of her;
   those who hold her fast are called blessed.

In order for us to live the Covenant life, what do we need? What is this? Why? With this wisdom, what will we be able to understand and approve? Why is this so important to us?

Read Philippians 1:3–11:

Thanksgiving and Prayer

3 I thank my God in all my remembrance of you, 4 always in every prayer of mine for you all making my prayer with joy, 5 because of your partnership in the gospel from the first day until now. 6 And I am sure of this, that he who began a good work in you will bring it to completion at the day of Jesus Christ. 7 It is right for me to feel this way about you all, because I hold you in my heart, for you are all partakers with me of grace,[a] both in my imprisonment and in the defense and confirmation of the gospel. 8 For God is my witness, how I yearn for you all with the affection of Christ Jesus. 9 And it is my prayer that your love may abound more and more, with knowledge and all discernment, 10 so that you may approve what is excellent, and so be pure and blameless for the day of Christ, 11 filled with the fruit of righteousness that comes through Jesus Christ, to the glory and praise of God.

____

____

____

____

____

If we are living this life of grace, what will we experience and when? What then can we expect and know if we are living in grace?

Read Acts 4:32–35:

They Had Everything in Common

32 Now the full number of those who believed were of one heart and soul, and no one said that any of the things that belonged to him was his own, but they had everything in common. 33 And with great power the apostles were giving their testimony to the resurrection of the Lord Jesus, and great grace was upon them all. 34 There was not a needy person among them, for as many as were owners of lands or houses sold them and brought the proceeds of what was sold 35 and laid it at the apostles' feet, and it was distributed to each as any had need.

When there is opposition to our life of grace, what can we still expect about experiencing the fullness of this life of grace? Why is that so important to us in the midst of these conflicts and opposition?

Read Acts 14:1–3:

Paul and Barnabas at Iconium
14 Now at Iconium they entered together into the Jewish synagogue and spoke in such a way that a great number of both Jews and Greeks believed. 2 But the unbelieving Jews stirred up the Gentiles and poisoned their minds against the brothers.[a] 3 So they remained for a long time, speaking boldly for the Lord, who bore witness to the word of his grace, granting signs and wonders to be done by their hands.

What is the mystery of Christ? What is His purpose of us experiencing His grace in us? What then are we to expect for our lives? Why?

> **Read Ephesians 3:1–7; 10–12:**
>
> The Mystery of the Gospel Revealed
> **3** For this reason I, Paul, a prisoner of Christ Jesus on behalf of you Gentiles— 2 assuming that you have heard of the stewardship of God's grace that was given to me for you, 3 how the mystery was made known to me by revelation, as I have written briefly. 4 When you read this, you can perceive my insight into the mystery of Christ, 5 which was not made known to the sons of men in other generations as it has now been revealed to his holy apostles and prophets by the Spirit. 6 This mystery is[a] that the Gentiles are fellow heirs, members of the same body, and partakers of the promise in Christ Jesus through the gospel.
>
> 7 Of this gospel I was made a minister according to the gift of God's grace, which was given me by the working of his power.

LESSON 3:
HOW DO WE RECEIVE/LIVE IN GRACE?

Grace is living in the Kingdom of God. Given this truth, what are we to be experiencing? When? Why is this so important to us?

> **Read Romans 14:17:**
>
> [17] For the kingdom of God is not a matter of eating and drinking but of righteousness and peace and joy in the Holy Spirit.

____

____

____

____

____

> "Grace is Him, and the life of grace is Him. This is not something arbitrary, rather, it is constant because it is His nature. "

Though we are believers and called to live in the Kingdom—in grace—what are the two consequences of not living in the Kingdom? What causes us to experience separation and falling from grace? Why then is this so important for how we live?

> **Read Galatians 5:1–4:**
>
> Christ Has Set Us Free
> **5** For freedom Christ has set us free; stand firm therefore, and do not submit again to a yoke of slavery.
>
> [2] Look: I, Paul, say to you that if you accept circumcision, Christ will be of no advantage to you. [3] I testify again to every man who accepts circumcision that he is obligated to keep the whole law. [4] You are severed from Christ, you who would be justified[a] by the law; you have fallen away from grace.

____

____

____

____

____

How else do we not experience His life of grace? What is the reason and the consequence of us engaging in disputing and arguing? How can we avoid this typical way of handling opposition and conflict?

> **Read James 4:1–10:**
>
> Warning Against Worldliness
> **4** What causes quarrels and what causes fights among you? Is it not this, that your passions[a] are at war within you?[b] 2 You desire and do not have, so you murder. You covet and cannot obtain, so you fight and quarrel. You do not have, because you do not ask. 3 You ask and do not receive, because you ask wrongly, to spend it on your passions. 4 You adulterous people![c] Do you not know that friendship with the world is enmity with God? Therefore whoever wishes to be a friend of the world makes himself an enemy of God. 5 Or do you suppose it is to no purpose that the Scripture says, "He yearns jealously over the spirit that he has made to dwell in us"? 6 But he gives more grace. Therefore it says, "God opposes the proud but gives grace to the humble." 7 Submit yourselves therefore to God. Resist the devil, and he will flee from you. 8 Draw near to God, and he will draw near to you. Cleanse your hands, you sinners, and purify your hearts, you double-minded. 9 Be wretched and mourn and weep. Let your laughter be turned to mourning and your joy to gloom. 10 Humble yourselves before the Lord, and he will exalt you.

____

____

____

____

____

LESSON 3:
HOW DO WE RECEIVE/LIVE IN GRACE?

In addition to conflict, what else causes us to exit the life of the Kingdom, the life of grace? What does that require on our part to return to Him and experience the fullness of grace? Why?

Read 1 Peter 5:2–7:

[2] shepherd the flock of God that is among you, exercising oversight,[a] not under compulsion, but willingly, as God would have you;[b] not for shameful gain, but eagerly; [3] not domineering over those in your charge, but being examples to the flock. [4] And when the chief Shepherd appears, you will receive the unfading crown of glory. [5] Likewise, you who are younger, be subject to the elders. Clothe yourselves, all of you, with humility toward one another, for "God opposes the proud but gives grace to the humble."

[6] Humble yourselves, therefore, under the mighty hand of God so that at the proper time he may exalt you, [7] casting all your anxieties on him, because he cares for you.

From the following three sets of verses, as we learn humility and surrender to God, what is the progression of surrender that we are to understand so we can truly know what it means to surrender; and what are the benefits of following this progression of surrender? What then do we need to understand about our role versus thinking freedom and holiness are automatic for believers?

Read Romans 6:4–7:

[4] We were buried therefore with him by baptism into death, in order that, just as Christ was raised from the dead by the glory of the Father, we too might walk in newness of life.

[5] For if we have been united with him in a death like his, we shall certainly be united with him in a resurrection like his. [6] We know that our old self[a] was crucified with him in order that the body of sin might be brought to nothing, so that we would no longer be enslaved to sin. [7] For one who has died has been set free[b] from sin.

____

____

____

____

____

Read Romans 6:8–18:

8 Now if we have died with Christ, we believe that we will also live with him. 9 We know that Christ, being raised from the dead, will never die again; death no longer has dominion over him. 10 For the death he died he died to sin, once for all, but the life he lives he lives to God. 11 So you also must consider yourselves dead to sin and alive to God in Christ Jesus.

12 Let not sin therefore reign in your mortal body, to make you obey its passions. 13 Do not present your members to sin as instruments for unrighteousness, but present yourselves to God as those who have been brought from death to life, and your members to God as instruments for righteousness. 14 For sin will have no dominion over you, since you are not under law but under grace.

Slaves to Righteousness

15 What then? Are we to sin because we are not under law but under grace? By no means! 16 Do you not know that if you present yourselves to anyone as obedient slaves,[a] you are slaves of the one whom you obey, either of sin, which leads to death, or of obedience, which leads to righteousness? 17 But thanks be to God, that you who were once slaves of sin have become obedient from the heart to the standard of teaching to which you were committed, 18 and, having been set free from sin, have become slaves of righteousness.

LESSON 3:
HOW DO WE RECEIVE/LIVE IN GRACE?

Read Romans 6:22:

[22] But now that you have been set free from sin and have become slaves of God, the fruit you get leads to sanctification and its end, eternal life.

____

____

____

____

____

How are we always to walk? If we do, what does He promise us? Why?

Read Psalm 26:3:

[3] For your steadfast love is before my eyes,
and I walk in your faithfulness.

____

____

____

____

____

To assist us in walking in His life of grace, what does God want us to do? Why? What are they to help us with?

> **Read Proverbs 13:20:**
>
> 20 Whoever walks with the wise becomes wise,
>   but the companion of fools will suffer harm.

____

____

____

____

____

In order to process together with wise people, what are we to do? When we do that, what is God doing? How then does this describe a new element of how we pray, and what we can expect from God as we do this?

> **Read Malachi 3:16–18:**
>
> The Book of Remembrance
> 16 Then those who feared the LORD spoke with one another. The LORD paid attention and heard them, and a book of remembrance was written before him of those who feared the LORD and esteemed his name. 17 "They shall be mine, says the LORD of hosts, in the day when I make up my treasured possession, and I will spare them as a man spares his son who serves him. 18 Then once more you shall see the distinction between the righteous and the wicked, between one who serves God and one who does not serve him.

____

____

____

____

____

Instead of engaging in people who oppose us, what are we to do with those who we consider wise? Why is this, and what does that mean then for how we live with others?

Read Romans 16:17–20:

Final Instructions and Greetings

[17] I appeal to you, brothers, to watch out for those who cause divisions and create obstacles contrary to the doctrine that you have been taught; avoid them. [18] For such persons do not serve our Lord Christ, but their own appetites,[a] and by smooth talk and flattery they deceive the hearts of the naive. [19] For your obedience is known to all, so that I rejoice over you, but I want you to be wise as to what is good and innocent as to what is evil. [20] The God of peace will soon crush Satan under your feet. The grace of our Lord Jesus Christ be with you.

What are we to seek and obtain with others who we consider wise? How do we fulfill this and experience the benefit of God's will and life of grace?

> **Read 2 Corinthians 13:11–14:**
>
> Final Greetings
> [11] Finally, brothers,[a] rejoice. Aim for restoration, comfort one another,[b] agree with one another, live in peace; and the God of love and peace will be with you. [12] Greet one another with a holy kiss. [13] All the saints greet you.
> [14] The grace of the Lord Jesus Christ and the love of God and the fellowship of the Holy Spirit be with you all.

____

____

____

____

If we pursue unity, with whom are we together seeking and receiving unity? What then is our focus? Why can we be assured we will have unity of the Spirit and His will when we are having others around us assist us with going to unity?

> **Read Ephesians 4:1–6:**
>
> Unity in the Body of Christ
> **4** I therefore, a prisoner for the Lord, urge you to walk in a manner worthy of the calling to which you have been called, [2] with all humility and gentleness, with patience, bearing with one another in love, [3] eager to maintain the unity of the Spirit in the bond of peace. [4] There is one body and one Spirit—just as you were called to the one hope that belongs to your call— [5] one Lord, one faith, one baptism, [6] one God and Father of all, who is over all and through all and in all.

LESSON 3:
HOW DO WE RECEIVE/LIVE IN GRACE?

____

____

____

____

____

As we seek unity, what is important for how we live? What does this mean, and how do we live in holiness?

Read 2 Peter 3:14–18:

Final Words

[14] Therefore, beloved, since you are waiting for these, be diligent to be found by him without spot or blemish, and at peace. [15] And count the patience of our Lord as salvation, just as our beloved brother Paul also wrote to you according to the wisdom given him, [16] as he does in all his letters when he speaks in them of these matters. There are some things in them that are hard to understand, which the ignorant and unstable twist to their own destruction, as they do the other Scriptures. [17] You therefore, beloved, knowing this beforehand, take care that you are not carried away with the error of lawless people and lose your own stability. [18] But grow in the grace and knowledge of our Lord and Savior Jesus Christ. To him be the glory both now and to the day of eternity. Amen.

____

____

____

____

____

To receive this life of holiness, what is our privilege to be with Christ and have dialogue with Him (prayer)? On what basis do we have this privilege? Why is that so important to us personally?

Read Hebrews 10:19–24:

The Full Assurance of Faith

[19] Therefore, brothers,[a] since we have confidence to enter the holy places by the blood of Jesus, [20] by the new and living way that he opened for us through the curtain, that is, through his flesh, [21] and since we have a great priest over the house of God, [22] let us draw near with a true heart in full assurance of faith, with our hearts sprinkled clean from an evil conscience and our bodies washed with pure water. [23] Let us hold fast the confession of our hope without wavering, for he who promised is faithful. [24] And let us consider how to stir up one another to love and good works,

____

____

____

____

____

LESSON 3:
HOW DO WE RECEIVE/LIVE IN GRACE?

When we are in trouble, having difficulty, or are not clear about His will, what are we to do? What then can we expect? Why is this so important to us living the life of grace in this difficult world?

> **Read Psalm 86:6–7:**
>
> 6 Give ear, O LORD, to my prayer;
>   listen to my plea for grace.
> 7 In the day of my trouble I call upon you,
>   for you answer me.

____

____

____

____

____

As we call out to God in our trouble, in our difficulty, what does He promise? What does this mean then for how we discover God's will and live out the life of grace? Why is this so important to how we practically follow His will?

> **Read Psalm 25:4–5:**
>
> 4 Make me to know your ways, O LORD;
>   teach me your paths.
> 5 Lead me in your truth and teach me,
>   for you are the God of my salvation;
>   for you I wait all the day long.

____

____

____

____

____

Read John 8:28–32:

28 So Jesus said to them, "When you have lifted up the Son of Man, then you will know that I am he, and that I do nothing on my own authority, but speak just as the Father taught me. 29 And he who sent me is with me. He has not left me alone, for I always do the things that are pleasing to him." 30 As he was saying these things, many believed in him.

The Truth Will Set You Free
31 So Jesus said to the Jews who had believed him, "If you abide in my word, you are truly my disciples, 32 and you will know the truth, and the truth will set you free."

____

____

____

____

____

From the following two sets of verses, since we are called to seek His will and follow Him in unity, what has He promised to give us to fulfill this? What does that mean for how we receive and follow?

Read Jeremiah 31:31–34:

The New Covenant
31 "Behold, the days are coming, declares the Lord, when I will make a new covenant with the house of Israel and the house of Judah, 32 not like the covenant that I made with their fathers on the day when I took them by the hand to bring them out of the land of Egypt, my covenant that they broke, though I was their husband, declares the LORD. 33 For this is the covenant that I will make with the house of Israel after those days, declares the LORD: I will put my law within them, and I will write it on their hearts. And I will be their

> God, and they shall be my people. [34] And no longer shall each one teach his neighbor and each his brother, saying, 'Know the LORD,' for they shall all know me, from the least of them to the greatest, declares the LORD. For I will forgive their iniquity, and I will remember their sin no more."

Read 1 John 2:24–27:

[24] Let what you heard from the beginning abide in you. If what you heard from the beginning abides in you, then you too will abide in the Son and in the Father. [25] And this is the promise that he made to us[a]—eternal life.

[26] I write these things to you about those who are trying to deceive you. [27] But the anointing that you received from him abides in you, and you have no need that anyone should teach you. But as his anointing teaches you about everything, and is true, and is no lie—just as it has taught you, abide in him.

What can we know about receiving His grace when we are in trouble or experiencing difficulty? How are we to approach this and seek His answers? What can we expect and why?

> **Read Psalm 34:14–19:**
>
> 14 Turn away from evil and do good;
>   seek peace and pursue it.
> 15 The eyes of the LORD are toward the righteous
>   and his ears toward their cry.
> 16 The face of the LORD is against those who do evil,
>   to cut off the memory of them from the earth.
> 17 When the righteous cry for help, the LORD hears
>   and delivers them out of all their troubles.
> 18 The LORD is near to the brokenhearted
>   and saves the crushed in spirit.
> 19 Many are the afflictions of the righteous,
>   but the LORD delivers him out of them all.

____

____

____

____

____

To live this out, what truth does God give us about the process? How does this work, and what can we expect? Why?

> **Read 2 Corinthians 9:6–15:**
>
> The Cheerful Giver
>
> [6] The point is this: whoever sows sparingly will also reap sparingly, and whoever sows bountifully[a] will also reap bountifully. [7] Each one must give as he has decided in his heart, not reluctantly or under compulsion, for God loves a cheerful giver. [8] And God is able to make all grace abound to you, so that having all sufficiency[b] in all things at all times, you may abound in every good work. [9] As it is written,
>
> "He has distributed freely, he has given to the poor;
>   his righteousness endures forever."
>
> [10] He who supplies seed to the sower and bread for food will supply and multiply your seed for sowing and increase the harvest of your righteousness. [11] You will be enriched in every way to be generous in every way, which through us will produce thanksgiving to God. [12] For the ministry of this service is not only supplying the needs of the saints but is also overflowing in many thanksgivings to God. [13] By their approval of this service, they[c] will glorify God because of your submission that comes from your confession of the gospel of Christ, and the generosity of your contribution for them and for all others, [14] while they long for you and pray for you, because of the surpassing grace of God upon you. [15] Thanks be to God for his inexpressible gift!

____

____

____

____

____

As we deal with difficult people—those who oppose us and come against us, what is important for us to understand about how we react to this? Why is this so important for us to remain in freedom and grace?

> **"...Christ Himself is grace. It's His nature all the time. It's not partial, once in a while, or every now and again. It is all the time."**

Read Galatians 5:13–26:

13 For you were called to freedom, brothers. Only do not use your freedom as an opportunity for the flesh, but through love serve one another. 14 For the whole law is fulfilled in one word: "You shall love your neighbor as yourself." 15 But if you bite and devour one another, watch out that you are not consumed by one another.

Keep in Step with the Spirit

16 But I say, walk by the Spirit, and you will not gratify the desires of the flesh. 17 For the desires of the flesh are against the Spirit, and the desires of the Spirit are against the flesh, for these are opposed to each other, to keep you from doing the things you want to do. 18 But if you are led by the Spirit, you are not under the law. 19 Now the works of the flesh are evident: sexual immorality, impurity, sensuality, 20 idolatry, sorcery, enmity, strife, jealousy, fits of anger, rivalries, dissensions, divisions, 21 envy,[a] drunkenness, orgies, and things like these. I warn you, as I warned you before, that those who do[b] such things will not inherit the kingdom of God. 22 But the fruit of the Spirit is love, joy, peace, patience, kindness, goodness, faithfulness, 23 gentleness, self-control; against such things there is no law. 24 And those who belong to Christ Jesus have crucified the flesh with its passions and desires.

25 If we live by the Spirit, let us also keep in step with the Spirit. 26 Let us not become conceited, provoking one another, envying one another.

____

____

____

____

____

Why is this all so important for us to remain in freedom and experience the full life of grace?

Read Romans 14:1–15:6:

Do Not Pass Judgment on One Another

14 As for the one who is weak in faith, welcome him, but not to quarrel over opinions. [2] One person believes he may eat anything, while the weak person eats only vegetables. [3] Let not the one who eats despise the one who abstains, and let not the one who abstains pass judgment on the one who eats, for God has welcomed him. [4] Who are you to pass judgment on the servant of another? It is before his own master[a] that he stands or falls. And he will be upheld, for the Lord is able to make him stand.

[5] One person esteems one day as better than another, while another esteems all days alike. Each one should be fully convinced in his own mind. [6] The one who observes the day, observes it in honor of the Lord. The one who eats, eats in honor of the Lord, since he gives thanks to God, while the one who abstains, abstains in honor of the Lord and gives thanks to God. [7] For none of us lives to himself, and none of us dies to himself. [8] For if we live, we live to the Lord, and if we die, we die to the Lord. So then, whether we live or whether we die, we are the Lord's. [9] For to this end Christ died and lived again, that he might be Lord both of the dead and of the living.

[10] Why do you pass judgment on your brother? Or you, why do you despise your brother? For we will all stand before the judgment seat of God; [11] for it is written,

"As I live, says the Lord, every knee shall bow to me,
    and every tongue shall confess[b] to God."
[12] So then each of us will give an account of himself to God.

Do Not Cause Another to Stumble

13 Therefore let us not pass judgment on one another any longer, but rather decide never to put a stumbling block or hindrance in the way of a brother. 14 I know and am persuaded in the Lord Jesus that nothing is unclean in itself, but it is unclean for anyone who thinks it unclean. 15 For if your brother is grieved by what you eat, you are no longer walking in love. By what you eat, do not destroy the one for whom Christ died. 16 So do not let what you regard as good be spoken of as evil. 17 For the kingdom of God is not a matter of eating and drinking but of righteousness and peace and joy in the Holy Spirit. 18 Whoever thus serves Christ is acceptable to God and approved by men. 19 So then let us pursue what makes for peace and for mutual upbuilding.

20 Do not, for the sake of food, destroy the work of God. Everything is indeed clean, but it is wrong for anyone to make another stumble by what he eats. 21 It is good not to eat meat or drink wine or do anything that causes your brother to stumble.[c] 22 The faith that you have, keep between yourself and God. Blessed is the one who has no reason to pass judgment on himself for what he approves. 23 But whoever has doubts is condemned if he eats, because the eating is not from faith. For whatever does not proceed from faith is sin.[d]

The Example of Christ

15 We who are strong have an obligation to bear with the failings of the weak, and not to please ourselves. 2 Let each of us please his neighbor for his good, to build him up. 3 For Christ did not please himself, but as it is written, "The reproaches of those who reproached you fell on me." 4 For whatever was written in former days was written for our instruction, that through endurance and through the encouragement of the Scriptures we might have hope. 5 May the God of endurance and encouragement grant you to live in such harmony with one another, in accord with Christ Jesus, 6 that together you may with one voice glorify the God and Father of our Lord Jesus Christ.

LESSON 4:
HOW DO WE GIVE AWAY GRACE?

In order to process these differences with other believers, how are we to discuss the differences with each other? What does that look like? Why is this so critical for how we handle all this?

> **Read Ephesians 4:15–16; 24–27:**
>
> [15] Rather, speaking the truth in love, we are to grow up in every way into him who is the head, into Christ, [16] from whom the whole body, joined and held together by every joint with which it is equipped, when each part is working properly, makes the body grow so that it builds itself up in love.
>
> [24] and to put on the new self, created after the likeness of God in true righteousness and holiness.
>
> [25] Therefore, having put away falsehood, let each one of you speak the truth with his neighbor, for we are members one of another. [26] Be angry and do not sin; do not let the sun go down on your anger, [27] and give no opportunity to the devil.

LESSON 4:
HOW DO WE GIVE AWAY GRACE?

When others continue to oppose us and are not willing to process truth together, what then are we called to do? What does this practically mean? What can we expect? Why is this so important for us to continue to live in freedom and a full life of grace?

Read Romans 12:9–20:

Marks of the True Christian

[9] Let love be genuine. Abhor what is evil; hold fast to what is good. [10] Love one another with brotherly affection. Outdo one another in showing honor. [11] Do not be slothful in zeal, be fervent in spirit,[a] serve the Lord. [12] Rejoice in hope, be patient in tribulation, be constant in prayer. [13] Contribute to the needs of the saints and seek to show hospitality.

[14] Bless those who persecute you; bless and do not curse them. [15] Rejoice with those who rejoice, weep with those who weep. [16] Live in harmony with one another. Do not be haughty, but associate with the lowly.[b] Never be wise in your own sight. [17] Repay no one evil for evil, but give thought to do what is honorable in the sight of all. [18] If possible, so far as it depends on you, live peaceably with all. [19] Beloved, never avenge yourselves, but leave it[c] to the wrath of God, for it is written, "Vengeance is mine, I will repay, says the Lord." [20] To the contrary, "if your enemy is hungry, feed him; if he is thirsty, give him something to drink; for by so doing you will heap burning coals on his head."

LESSON 4:
HOW DO WE GIVE AWAY GRACE?

In our freedom, we are always called to offer our peace. What does that mean for those who are opposing us? What do we do if they agree to this offer? What do we do if they do not accept this offer? In both of their reactions, why can we continue to live in freedom and experience the full life of grace?

Read Luke 10:1–13:

Jesus Sends Out the Seventy-Two

10 After this the Lord appointed seventy-two[a] others and sent them on ahead of him, two by two, into every town and place where he himself was about to go. 2 And he said to them, "The harvest is plentiful, but the laborers are few. Therefore pray earnestly to the Lord of the harvest to send out laborers into his harvest. 3 Go your way; behold, I am sending you out as lambs in the midst of wolves. 4 Carry no moneybag, no knapsack, no sandals, and greet no one on the road. 5 Whatever house you enter, first say, 'Peace be to this house!' 6 And if a son of peace is there, your peace will rest upon him. But if not, it will return to you. 7 And remain in the same house, eating and drinking what they provide, for the laborer deserves his wages. Do not go from house to house. 8 Whenever you enter a town and they receive you, eat what is set before you. 9 Heal the sick in it and say to them, 'The kingdom of God has come near to you.' 10 But whenever you enter a town and they do not receive you, go into its streets and say, 11 'Even the dust of your town that clings to our feet we wipe off against you. Nevertheless, know this, that the kingdom of God has come near.' 12 I tell you, it will be more bearable on that day for Sodom than for that town.

Woe to Unrepentant Cities

13 "Woe to you, Chorazin! Woe to you, Bethsaida! For if the mighty works done in you had been done in Tyre and Sidon, they would have repented long ago, sitting in sackcloth and ashes.

____

____

____

____

____

LESSON 4:
HOW DO WE GIVE AWAY GRACE?

As we consider grace, one of our purposes within the body of Christ is to do what? What does that truly mean as we now understand grace? What will be the benefit to them and the benefit to us? How does this impact our life of freedom and grace?

Read Romans 12:3–8:

Gifts of Grace

[3] For by the grace given to me I say to everyone among you not to think of himself more highly than he ought to think, but to think with sober judgment, each according to the measure of faith that God has assigned. [4] For as in one body we have many members,[a] and the members do not all have the same function, [5] so we, though many, are one body in Christ, and individually members one of another. [6] Having gifts that differ according to the grace given to us, let us use them: if prophecy, in proportion to our faith; [7] if service, in our serving; the one who teaches, in his teaching; [8] the one who exhorts, in his exhortation; the one who contributes, in generosity; the one who leads,[b] with zeal; the one who does acts of mercy, with cheerfulness.

____

____

____

____

____

LESSON 4:
HOW DO WE GIVE AWAY GRACE?

As we serve others, our call is to also identify and walk with others who will then do what? Why is this so important to fulfilling God's bigger purpose? Why is this so important for us to live this way?

Read 2 Timothy 2:1–7:

A Good Soldier of Christ Jesus

2 You then, my child, be strengthened by the grace that is in Christ Jesus, [2] and what you have heard from me in the presence of many witnesses entrust to faithful men,[a] who will be able to teach others also. [3] Share in suffering as a good soldier of Christ Jesus. [4] No soldier gets entangled in civilian pursuits, since his aim is to please the one who enlisted him. [5] An athlete is not crowned unless he competes according to the rules. [6] It is the hard-working farmer who ought to have the first share of the crops. [7] Think over what I say, for the Lord will give you understanding in everything.

9 7 9 8 2 1 8 2 4 4 7 0 5